Bookkeeping and Business:

For Your AVON Business for the 20/21 Tax Year

ELYSE BURNS-HILL

Edition 1
First Published June 2020

Contact Address: Elyse Burns-Hill, C/O ElysianIsland Equities Ltd, Wessex House, Eastleigh, Hampshire, SO50 9FD

DISCLAIMER: Please do not take this book or associated videos as any form of personal tax advice. I do not know your personal tax situation and therefore cannot advise what is the best course of action. You take full responsibility for completing and submitting your Self-Assessment Tax Return.

Table of Contents

ABOUT THE AUTHOR
Elyse Burns-Hill

Elyse is a qualified Accountant and full member of the Association of Chartered Certified Accountants (ACCA). She started her Accountancy career at pwc in Malta in 2010 and has also practiced in firms in Jersey and Hampshire. She is now Associate Director at SGW Accountants and Business Advisors, pending full Director once her Practicing Certificate has been granted by her professional body (expected late 2020).

Elyse is a mummy of 2 little girls born 2016 and 2019, and she joined AVON as a representative in 2016 as a way to integrate into the community a bit after her first baby was born and she was stuck at home feeling a little lonely. She decided to use her accounting skills for good in 2017 when she started the free Facebook group as she realised there were so many questions and so little help out there for Reps. These books follow on from the group.

Facebook Support Groups:

Elyse runs several support groups through Facebook. The links are available through the website www.selfassessment4.co.uk and also through the Self-Assessment 4 Facebook page: www.facebook.com/selfassessment4

Other Business Interests:

As well as her Accountancy practice, Elyse is also:

- Co-Owner and Director of The Inspire Network, providing networking opportunities and training for business-women in the UK;
- Co-Director and Treasurer of Collabor8 – People in Business CIC, a social enterprise aimed to support and signpost people in business to training and funding;
- Chair of the Board of Directors of Dandelion Healthcare, a growing organisation that will raise the standards of mental healthcare in the UK;
- Treasurer of The Dandelion Fellowship, a charity that raises money to help fund mental healthcare for people who are unable to get help through the NHS and are unable to fund themselves privately or through insurance.

Publications:

Bookkeeping & Business: For Your AVON Business for the 19/20 Tax Year	(April 2019)
Bookkeeping & Business: For Your AVON Business for the 20/21 Tax Year	(June 2020)
Bookkeeping Your Sole Trader Business for the 20/21 Tax Year	(July 2020)
14 Steps to Achieving Financial Success in Your Business	(July 2020)
21 Steps To Becoming a Time Lady	(September 2020)

All Available through Amazon.co.uk

INTRODUCTION TO THE BOOK
Bookkeeping & Business

This book is relevant to all AVON Sales Representatives and Sales Leaders, new and seasoned. I'd also recommend joining my free Facebook group called "Self Assessment 4 Avon Reps" as a partner to this book. If you look in the Units section in the group, you will see that each unit corresponds with the chapters in this book. The book does stand-alone but if you are struggling with understanding anything, the group may have additional videos or explanations that will help you.

If you aren't on Facebook and need a little extra guidance, please email the team at: bookquestions@selfassessment4.co.uk.

Chapter 1
If you are new to AVON and new to Self-Employment, you will want to read the first chapter on 'Keeping Records and Registration'. This is formatted as a question and answer so you can easily find the information you need.

Chapter 2
Chapter two is all about setting financial goals for your AVON business and creating a plan to achieve them. Whether you want to have a little extra income on the side, or you intend building your AVON business to become a full-time income for you and your family, you still need to have your goals and plans in place!

Chapter 3
There are a lot of things to think about when you are running a business, and even more if you are also running a household, raising a family and/or holding down employment. We could all do a bit more to ensure we spend our time productively and efficiently. So Chapter three covers a few ways you can help yourself to be a little more organised and productive.

Chapter 4
I'm not going to teach you all there is to know about bookkeeping, I'm going to teach you 'just enough' to help you achieve your goal – to be able to submit your tax return on your own. Chapter 4 runs through all the things that you will need to include in the 2 numbers you are looking to create; your total sales and your total expenses.

Chapter 5
The last step to completing your Self-Assessment is to complete the form. It's a big form! So I've broken it down, taken screenshots and explained what I can in text and each section also has a link to a video so you can watch me go through that part of the form.

Chapter 6
You are armed with all the info, in this chapter I have provided you with a load of blank forms to record all your numbers from your order forms, invoices and receipts. There is a spreadsheet you can download for free through the Facebook group (or contact the

team at the email address above) or if you'd like to stick with pen and paper, use these forms.

Don't get overwhelmed!
Bookkeeping, Tax, Self-Assessment – it's all scary stuff when you are just starting out, and it can be enough to turn a lot of people away from Self-Employment. I started the Facebook groups and have now produced these books as a way to make this side of your business as easy as possible for you.

When you get a little overwhelmed by how much there is to do, just stop, step back and re-ground yourself.

Remember:

- you only need to create 2 numbers – your total sales and your total expenses;
- HMRC are not going to fine the pants off you if you get it wrong – they know you are not an accountant and might make mistakes. They do want to see you trying the best you can.

How to access all the videos linked in the book

Please go to: www.selfassessment4.com/20-21-avon-videos

You will be asked to complete checkout, but please use the following code to complete the checkout process: **AVON2021-fxgn37**

You will then be asked to create a login and taken to where you can access the videos.

CHECKLIST FOR NEWBIES

one by one...

- ☐ Read "Introduction To The Book" (page before this one!)
- ☐ If you are on Facebook; join the group so that you can ask questions
- ☐ Register for access to the videos on the website (see page 7 for how to do this)
- ☐ Read Chapter 1
- ☐ Register as Self-Employed with HMRC and *make a note of your login:*

  Government Gateway ______________________________

  Password ____

  (<u>Please</u> make sure you keep this login safe!)
- ☐ Activate your Self-Assessment on your Government Gateway Account
- ☐ Find a folder/box to keep all your financial records and this book safely
- ☐ Use the pages in Chapter 6 to calculate your *income* on a single campaign
- ☐ Use the pages in Chapter 6 to calculate your *expenses* on a single campaign
- ☐ Rinse and repeat each campaign
- ☐ Using each Campaign sheet, complete the summary page
- ☐ Sign into your Government Gateway Account after the end of the tax year and complete your tax return using the guide in chapter 5.
- ☐ Reward yourself!

CHAPTER 1

Record Keeping and Registration

I decided that the format for this chapter would probably be best as a question and answer so that you can easily find the information you need. If you have any other questions that are not covered here, please feel free to pop into the Facebook group and ask.

What records do I need to keep?

You'll need to keep all your Avon invoices and Sales Leader statements.

You will also need to keep receipts and invoices of any business purchases you make from any other supplier (e.g Vistaprint if you have business cards or leaflets printed, or you buy baskets to make gift baskets etc).

If you need to drive in the car to deliver orders or visit new reps on your team, you'll need to keep a log of all your mileage (there's a log in Chapter 7).

You should be keeping order forms or at least some proof of sales. If you run a market stall, you could just keep a list of your sales and how much was spent.

Do I need to submit all my records to HMRC?

No, you don't need to submit any of your records, you just complete the Self-Assessment form with the numbers that you have calculated and submit that. If HMRC ever want to review your records so that they can check that your Self-Assessment was accurate, they will contact you and arrange to view your records. (It's unlikely that will happen, but you do need to be ready just in case).

How long do I need to keep my records?

You will need to keep your records for

Why do I need to register with HMRC?

When you first register with Avon, you become a Self-Employed Sales Representative. This means you have responsibility to return information to HMRC regarding your earnings so that you can be taxed properly.

Some people argue that if you are only planning on selling to friends and family that you are not running a business. My response to that is that you are running a business, and therefore you need to register.

The only possible time that you MAY not need to be registered is if you have a Rep account in order to buy only for yourself – in that situation your sales figure will be £0 as you haven't sold on any of the product that you have purchased. You will then be able to claim the trading allowance and not need to submit a return (unless you have any other income outside of employment that should be returned through Self-Assessment).

When do I need to register as Self-Employed with HMRC?

You must register with HMRC no later than 5th October in your business's second tax year, otherwise you could be fined.

So, what does that mean?

If you started Avon between 6 April 2020 and 5 April 2021, you need to have registered by 5 October 2021.

However, I would advise you don't leave it to the last minute...register as soon as you can so that it's done.

How do I register as Self Employed with HMRC?

The easiest way to register for Self-Employment is to use the online form: https://www.gov.uk/log-in-file-self-assessment-tax-return/register-if-youre-self-employed

When you register you will:

- create a government gateway login (make sure you keep a note of your login – it's easy to forget as you only use it once a year!)

- get a letter with your 10-digit Unique Taxpayer Reference (UTR)

- be enrolled for the Self-Assessment online service once you have activated the service using the activation code you will receive by letter within 10 days of registration.

What if I am beyond the deadline for registering as Self Employed?

Give HMRC a call.

They are generally not a problem if you go to them and say you didn't realise you had to register, you bought a book or joined a group on Facebook and found out that you should have been registered and you've given them a call straight away.

Don't take that as gospel, but if THEY find that you've been running a business without registering, then they will likely impose penalties.

If you self-declare that you should have been registered but weren't, you will get into a lot less trouble!

They will probably ask you when you started as an AVON Rep (so make sure you have that date ready) and ask you to complete however many returns you should have completed by this point.

Do I still need to submit a return if I've earnt less than £1000?

The answer, in the majority of circumstances...is yes, you will. Let's look at this in more depth:

History:

This allowance was first announced a few years ago for the 16/17 tax year, but then was put on the bench because of Brexit. It's now come back into force again and has been applicable from the 17/18 tax year.

The Important Points:

The £1000 is turnover, not profit. Just to give you an idea, if you sell £55 worth of products every campaign for a year – you're pretty much at that limit - £55 x 18 camps = £990.

If your turnover is below £1000 (possibly will be if you are a new rep and have only done a few campaigns in the year) you don't have to register for self-assessment in order to claim it - unless you already need to be registered for another reason.

If you are already registered, but still qualify for the allowance, you can use it on your self-assessment INSTEAD of claiming your business expenses. You will still need to keep records showing your turnover...i.e all your order forms and any other receipts from ebay/markets etc.

If you are employed and you sell to your boss, then you disqualify yourself from claiming the allowance. Colleagues are ok, but not your boss.

If you have multiple sources of self-employed income (eg you are an AVON rep AND have a crafty business or Scentsy etc), this £1000 is across the board for ALL your self-employed income - not for each one.

If you qualify for the allowance, but look like you are going to make a loss for the year with your income less all your claimable expenses, you will be better off registering the loss so you can offset it against future profits rather than claiming the allowance.

If you want to be able to pay class 2 NI contributions, you will need to register and submit the self-assessment.

If you want to claim Tax Free Childcare for childcare costs based on your self-employment income you will need to register and submit the self-assessment.

If you want to claim Maternity Allowance, based on your self-employment income you will need to register and submit the self-assessment.

Conclusion:

Most of you will still be needing to register and submit your tax returns.

Here's the link to the Government Info Page so you can check it out for yourself: https://www.gov.uk/guidance/tax-free-allowances-on-property-and-trading-income#trade

I've also created a video covering the above information – you can watch it on YouTube here: https://youtu.be/UJedUd0-o3k

CHAPTER 2
Financial Goals For Your AVON Business

FIVE reasons why it's really important to set your financial goals:

#1 Where are you going?

What do you consider to be successful? Are you achieving what you set out to achieve? Setting financial goals will help you answer both these questions. Your answers will be different from the next person, they are solely based on your situation. Once you figure out what you need to achieve, i.e £100 per month, £500 per month or £1000 per month, you can then decide how you are going to achieve it. Which brings us on to our next point:

#2 Different financial goals require different strategies

A small "extra spending money" goal will require a different level of effort and a different plan to achieve than a "saving up to buy a house" type goal. If you are hoping to use the money from your Avon business to buy a new house, you will really have to prioritise the money-making activities, and make sure you are spending time to your best advantage.

#3 Setting financial goals help you stay focused

There's a reason for the phrase "keeping your eye on the prize"! It helps you stay laser focused on what you are there to do. Yes, it's fun messing around with the pretty pictures for your Avon group, but is it providing value? To your customers, your potential customers, and to your business? If the answer is no, you probably need to find something more productive to focus on. On the other hand, if your financial goals aren't that big and you are doing it to meet more people in your local community and have a bit of extra spending money, then spend your time doing pretty pictures if that's what you enjoy.

#4 You can find the right tools to help

If you are serious about making money with your AVON business, there are many tools out there that can help you. For example, ClickFunnels – this is a piece of software that can help you create an online sales process. This can really help with things like recruiting new members into your team. The normal price of this is $97 per month, but that isn't a big investment for your business to make if it helps you convert 4 times as many people into reps joining your team.

Obviously, I'm not advocating that you go and pay the $97 per month without doing your research and training to make sure you can use it to your best advantage.
There are also other free tools that can help, for example, Canva for creating free images to share.

Knowing what your goals are will help you critically evaluate the tools available and whether it will help you achieve them.

#5 Setting financial goals creates a sense of achievement

Setting your goals is the first step towards achieving them. The journey isn't always easy, but that is what makes the sense of achievement all the greater when you get there.

How to set my financial goals

You may have heard of SMART goals?
Well, my wonderful other half (who is a clinical psychologist) has been busy writing a book articulating his new approach for the last year.

It is called the SMARTER-life-GROWTH approach; he brings together clinical psychology, positive psychology and coaching principles to create a framework to help you create a better life. I'm currently working on re-working this personal growth material into a book about business growth (with Pat's help!).

So, the upshot of it all is to make SMARTER goals:

Specific
Measurable
Achievable
Relevant
Time bound
Evaluation
Reflection

So, let's work through an example, and then we'll work through one for you to fill in the blanks:

Example goal

Specific
A good way to approach this is to answer the 5 "W" questions:
What do I want to accomplish?
Why is this goal important?
Who is involved?
Where is it located?
Which resources are involved?

"I want to gain the skills and experience necessary to become a top 100 Avon Rep and Sales Leader so that I can lead a great team and pursue some worthy causes."

Measurable
This would seem to be one of the easier parts to complete as it's all about your actual income goals. However, you also want to think about what Peter Drucker (1909 – 2005), a management guru once said: "what gets measured, gets managed". The easiest way to explain this is with an example:

If I say my goal is to achieve £250 in profit in a month, (assuming I'm getting 25% commission and there are no other costs involved – just to keep the numbers simple), then I'm looking at needing to achieve about £1000 worth of orders.

We could take one of several routes to achieve that; one could be 200 orders averaging £5 per order, and many of these might be one off orders because of a social media special offer you did on a particular product.

Another route could be having built up an engaged audience on Facebook (for example), and you have about 50 people who would buy from you most campaigns. Because they are also very keen on the content that you give out, their average order value is about £20.

As you can probably see, the first option would be much easier to achieve in the short term, however, is unlikely to be sustainable. It is much harder to be finding and selling to new customers every campaign.

The second option will take much longer to build up, and some thought will be needed to provide meaningful content to your loyal customers, but the payoff is that you have fewer orders to process, and less actual sales activity to do (these customers are already sold – you just need to put the right offer in front of them and they'll buy).

So, if we go back to Mr Drucker's statement; "what gets measured, gets managed"; if we focus on average order value, rather than our total income goal, we would be looking to get that as high as possible, so that we can reduce the number of total orders. Over time, this approach will provide us with more time for other profit focused activities, thereby allowing us to grow the business.

"My profit goal is £250 per campaign, with an average order value of at least £20"

Achievable
This is all about making sure you have the resources and the ability to achieve the goal you are setting. If you have 20 hours available each week to put into your Avon business, then make sure you are being realistic with your goal. If your goal will require a 40 hour week minimum, you might be stretching a little bit too far with your goal!

The other thing to consider is your ability to achieve it, i.e. is it within your control. For example, "signing up 10 new reps this month" is not actually within your control, you might find the leads, but you have no control over whether they will signup…that's a limitation of being human!!

You would be better to set your goal as "attracting and discussing the opportunity with 15 leads this month". You might convert 1 person, you might convert all 15, but at least you have control over the attracting leads.

"I will work on attracting 15 new engaged potential customers into my Facebook group this month."

Relevant
There are several levels of goals, you might have short term, medium term and long term goals, whether they are written out and planned or not. What we are looking for with being relevant, is about making sure that there is consistency in your short, medium and long term goals.

So, if you have a medium term goal of earning £1500 per month with your Avon business, but your short term goals are starting a family and working towards achieving the promotion at your full time job, then you can see there is a bit of incongruence there.

It's tiring being pregnant and hard enough to be working a full time job, without trying to build up a business as well. In fact, trying to achieve a promotion while pregnant might also be difficult – not many bosses will be open minded enough to let that happen!

"My short and medium term plans all take me towards the ultimate long term goal, which is to buy a house and support the purchase with a monthly income of £1500"

Time bound
This one is an easy one – set a deadline for your goal. If you don't have a time limit on it, it's easy to leave until tomorrow.

"I will be earning my target of £250 per campaign by 1 August 2020"

Evaluation
Constantly evaluate your performance. Are the tasks that you are doing helping you to work towards your goal? If not, why not? Do you need more training to help you achieve more? Is this task just not working out for you, so you should change your approach?

For example, posting on your Avon Business Facebook page and getting no engagement or responses from people. You might just need to make some tweaks, like making sure your page is linked on your personal profile, that you've shared it with friends and family, that you are posting other things and not just sales posts all the time. Learning some of these techniques might help you increase engagement on your page.

On the other hand, maybe a Facebook page just doesn't work for you. Maybe you need to change your approach and go for a Facebook Group instead. Facebook have different algorithms and other fancy stuff going on behind the scenes that mean that different things get different priorities. You just have to experiment and see what works for you.

Of course, you need to be evaluating your performance on all levels; social media engagement, number of orders, average order value etc. Keep a journal, and record what you do and their outcomes. That way you can focus on what works for you and what doesn't...and focus more on the stuff that works.

"Every week I will sit and evaluate my performance and figure out what helps me to achieve my goal"

Reflection
Reflection is what would be done at the end when you have achieved your goal. Look back at the work you did to achieve it, and see what you could have done differently. Very often we only see things in hindsight, not when we are in the middle of it. So, taking time to look back over your actions may provide some insight that you would otherwise have missed.

Free tip: Make sure you write down your lessons; it will help you articulate exactly what you mean, and ensure you don't forget it and make the same mistake again next time!

"I will reflect upon my actions when I have achieved my goal to see if there are any lessons to learn"

Conclusion
Let's put it all together so that we can see it all in one place. (I've tweaked it slightly from the examples given above so that it hangs together a bit better).

- *I want to gain the skills and experience necessary to become a high earning Avon rep and Sales Leader so that I can lead a great team and pursue some worthy causes;*
- *My first profit goal is £250 per campaign, with an average order value of at least £20;*
- *I will work on attracting 15 new engaged potential customers into my Facebook group each campaign;*
- *My short and medium term goals all take me towards the ultimate long term goal, which is to buy a house and support the purchase with a monthly income of £1500;*
- *I will be earning my target of £250 per campaign by 1 August 2020.*
- *Every week I will sit and evaluate my performance and figure out what helps me to achieve my goal;*
- *I will reflect upon my actions when I have achieved my goal to see if there are any lessons to learn.*

My Goal Worksheet

Specific
(what, why, who, where, which)

Measurable
(what gets measured gets managed)

Achievable
(do you have the resources and ability)

Relevant
(goal congruence)

Timely
(set yourself a deadline)

Evaluate
(constant evaluation)

Reflect
(take time to inspect your hindsight for any lessons)

In conclusion:
(write all the parts of your goal together)

How to achieve your financial goals

The second part of the SMARTER-life-GROWTH approach is about creating a plan to achieve those SMARTER goals. And it goes like this:

Goals
Reality
Options
Way forward
Tactics
Habit

Again, we'll work our way through an example together, and then I'll guide you through a blank version for you to build your plan.

Example Plan

Goals
We've already worked on creating your goals in the previous section – if you haven't done that yet, I'd advise going back and working on your goals before getting going on this section.

So, as a reminder, our goal from the previous section is:

- *I want to gain the skills and experience necessary to become a top earning Avon rep and Sales Leader so that I can lead a great team and pursue some worthy causes;*
- *My first profit goal is £250 per campaign, with an average order value of at least £20;*
- *I will work on attracting 15 new engaged potential customers into my Facebook group each campaign;*
- *My short and medium term goals all take me towards the ultimate long term goal, which is to buy a house and support the purchase with a monthly income of £1500;*
- *I will be earning my target of £250 per campaign by 1 August 2020.*
- *Every week I will sit and evaluate my performance and figure out what helps me to achieve my goal;*
- *I will reflect upon my actions when I have achieved my goal to see if there are any lessons to learn.*

Reality
This is about establishing where you are right now in relation to your goal. Try to line it up with some of the aspects of your goal:

"I am earning on average £30 per campaign and my average order value is £6. I am attracting about 5 potential customers into my group each month, but they don't seem very engaged".

Options
We want to see what options we have that will help us achieve our goals, and this is a two-step process. The first step is to perform a SWOT analysis – if you haven't heard of it before, don't panic – it's really not too difficult to get your head around. The second step is to use your SWOT analysis to identify several options that will help you achieve your goal.

SWOT Analysis:
SWOT stands for Strengths, Weaknesses, Opportunities and Threats. So, all you need to think about is your personal strengths and weaknesses when it comes to doing business, and any opportunities and threats there may be to the industry, to Avon, to your locality etc. Let's look at an example:

STRENGTHS	**WEAKNESSES**
Pretty good with Facebook Enjoy putting videos together Good at researching topics Good with the computer	Social anxiety Messy handwriting
I can set up a personalised address for my Avon store I have good availability in the evening when kids are in bed	There are a LOT of Avon reps in my local area My availability is not particularly good during the day due to childcare
OPPORTUNITIES	**THREATS**

I've given you a few fairly basic ideas above, and you can probably see where I'm going with it. Be creative with completing your SWOT analysis and take your time doing it – what I've written above could easily relate to half the reps out there. Think of other things to include and don't be afraid to Google for inspiration, or ask friends "what do you think my strengths are?".

The next stage is to come up with several options based on what you wrote in your SWOT analysis.

For example:

1. *I could look for a new area and deliver books to those addresses. Talking to people in the post office, the shops and in my local community about my business will help me get new customers.*

2. *I could focus my efforts online and leveraging my abilities with Facebook.*

Way Forward
At this stage, we look at the different options we have in front of us, and decide which will be the best/fastest/cheapest/most likely to succeed.

Depending on the type of person you are, a simple pro & con list might be the best way to decide. Or go with your heart, one option will seem exciting and motivating, while another will make you feel tired before you even start.

Option 1
Pros: This is the standard way that reps do and have always done Avon, so there will be lots of people to ask when I get stuck.
Cons: Social anxiety, availability not good during the day or early evening, *social anxiety*, messy hand writing, *social anxiety (!!)* and lots of reps in the area.

Option 2
Pros: Good with Facebook, I enjoy putting videos together and sharing my passion for make-up, more people are online during the evening, so that fits with my availability, I can make use of Avon's option to use the online store.
Cons: There are a lot of other reps competing for attention online, so I will have to think of something different and unique so that I can be noticed.

"My way forward is to focus on selling Avon online"

Tactics
Way forward is big picture, strategy – the direction you are going to go with your business. Tactics is more about creating a step by step plan to make that happen. This part will also help with your reflections at the end; if you have written down your step by step guide, then you can use it as an aide memoire to help you identify any weak areas of your process.

Flesh this out in as much detail as you can, I'll put a superficial plan below, but you will want something much more in depth for your business.

1. *Create a Facebook group and update my profile to include a link to my group, make sure there are some public posts that would display my interest in Avon and change my cover photo to something that supports my business.*
2. *Post to my group twice daily, and over the week, the split of posts will be 5 sales posts in every 14 posts. The other posts will be either sharing other people's interesting content, creating tutorials or little images with quotes or pretty pictures with the aim of increasing engagement.*
3. *To acquire more group members, I will share some tutorials etc into Business and Selling groups on Facebook with a link back to my group.*

etc...

Habits
Any part of your plan that involves repetitive actions will be MUCH easier if you create a habit around doing it.

For example, if you plan to post to your Facebook group twice every day, then choose an activity that you do twice a day, that will act as a trigger to remind you to post. It could be brushing your teeth; brush your teeth and it reminds you to go and open your laptop and post something interesting to your group. Or if you've already pre-prepared your images, you could sit on the toilet after you've done your teeth (with the lid down...I'm not suggesting anything else...although you can if you want!!) and post from your phone.

Have a look back at your tactics plan and see what repetitive items you could create a habit around.

Here's a link to an article about habit forming that I think is just brilliant. I was going to write this section in more depth, but I think this article just says it all! https://jamesclear.com/habit-guide

My Goal Planning Worksheet

Goals
(reminder)

Reality
(reminder)

Options

(SWOT analysis and then work out what option you have from there)

STRENGTHS	**WEAKNESSES**
OPPORTUNITIES	**THREATS**

Way forward
(best of your options)

Tactics
(detailed task list following your Way Forward)

Habits
(what repetitive actions could you create habits out of?)

How to Develop a Prosperity Mindset

Having a prosperity mindset is a key factor in reaching your financial goals. It keeps you on track toward your goals regardless of any challenges you encounter along the way.

These strategies below will help you foster a prosperity mindset that can enable you to live the life you desire.

Keep Your Focus
If you find that your mind wanders from idea to idea, create one set plan and stick to it. In your plan, create a list of specific achievable action steps that lead to your goal, and then work on at least one task each day to help maintain your focus.

Plan for Success
It doesn't matter how focused you are if you don't have a proper plan. Your financial goals aren't going to happen just by deciding on a number. Make some clear plans on how you're going to get there – all you need to do is follow the instruction in the previous section. This will get you past the *dream phase* so you can start making your ultimate goals a reality.

Be as detailed in your plan as possible and set each task as a mini-goal. Achieving these small goals daily keeps you motivated and moving along toward your big goal.

Model Yourself After Successful People
One of the best decisions you can make is to use other successful people as your role models. Think about what you admire about these people and then try to model their behaviour.

You'll also want to study the reasons why they've become successful. How do you think they got to where they are? Can you embark on a similar journey? Chances are that you can; all you need to do is build up the courage to achieve.

Believe in Yourself

Unfortunately, too many people don't have confidence in their abilities and they fail to try or give up far too quickly. You don't have to be one of these people!

Look back at the people you admire and you'll likely notice that they felt like giving up at some point. But they didn't! They likely have an unwavering belief in their abilities and a drive to succeed, no matter what.

You *can* reach your financial goals! Believe that it *is* possible! People have proven that it's possible, and ***you can achieve anything that's possible.***

Pay It Forward

Along your journey to success, you can practise good karma by paying it forward. Spread your knowledge so that others can learn the lessons you've learned. You can serve as a mentor to others just like you were mentored when you were starting out.

When you are kind to others, that kindness will find its way right back to you. You never know what good can come out of some simple kindness.

It may take some time and effort to develop your prosperity mindset, but the rewards are well worth it. Once you've mastered it, it will be with you for the rest of your life, guiding you to achieve any financial goals you desire.

CHAPTER 3
Productivity and Time Management

Overcome Procrastination With Mini-Tasks

Do you ever procrastinate? Would you like to put a stop to this time-wasting habit? You can make progress today by breaking your to-do list into mini-tasks.

Here's how it works:

A mini-task is a task that is so small you couldn't make it any smaller without being silly about it. Posting on an Avon Facebook Group to ask a specific question would be a good example of a mini-task.

In general, mini-tasks take 15 minutes or less to accomplish.

This time management technique addresses one of the most common causes of procrastination on larger projects: uncertainty about where to get started. For example, writing a book is a sequence of achievable tasks, but people frequently have a difficult time even getting started on such a seemingly huge project.

Ideally, you'd plan the entire process from beginning to end. This may not always be possible; some projects have too much uncertainty to be able to predict the entire process from the beginning. But you could still develop a task list for as far as you're able to see. At some point, you'll be able to see further down the path and can develop new mini-tasks.

Let's use a simple example: Setting up your Facebook Page for Customers
(I've filled this out a bit with more info on the marketing side as I know this will be helpful for some people!)

1. Decide who your ideal customer would be.
   Maybe you decide you want to focus on people who want to buy perfume.

2. Write up your Avatar to deep dive into your ideal customer.
   Who they are, where they hang out etc. There's plenty of exercises around to take you through creating an Avatar step by step if you Google it

3. Create an image for your profile picture
   Make sure it shows your face and would appeal to your ideal customer. Canva is a great product to use for this.

4. Create a cover image for your page.
   Make sure it shows the personality of your business, and even if you use it to showcase a different offer each campaign, try to keep the basic look the same, so that people recognise it when they come to your page.

5. Create a posting schedule for the next campaign.
   Don't just plan sales posts, look at what other pages to do increase engagement and adapt to work for you and your audience.

6. Create some content to post for now.
   When you share your page, it will need to have some content on it.

7. Update your profile to show your page.
   People on Facebook are nosy, they will visit your profile to see who you are and what you do. If you don't have your page on your profile, you may be missing out on new customers, as they will click through to your page if they are interested.

8. Share your page.
   Ask friends and family to like it (and to drop some emoji's on your posts to help them show more engagement – FB likes to see engagement, and will organically show your posts to more people). Plenty of small business groups do "Following threads" usually on a Friday or Saturday – make sure you post your page in these threads and like other people's pages back too.

Number 5 might still seem like a huge job, so you could break it down even further:

1. Find a posting schedule download from the internet.
2. Look at 3 of my favourite pages to see the type of things they post and what gets the most engagement. Write notes about the themes that I notice.
3. Fill in my plan for the next campaign.
4. Create 3 new posts on Monday and schedule to post on Monday, Tuesday and Wednesday at 6pm.
5. Create 3 new posts on Tuesday and schedule to post on Thursday, Friday and Saturday at 6pm.

And so on.

A good rule of thumb is that if the thought of completing the task fills you with dread, you might feel less daunted if you break your process down into smaller tasks.

More Benefits of Mini-Task Lists

A list of mini-tasks is like a recipe; all you have to do is move down the list. When you get to the end, you're done. *None of the tasks should take a lot of time or be so complex that you're hesitant to complete the step.*

An added benefit of making such a list is that you'll have an excellent idea of how long the overall project will take. Assigning an accurate time estimate without having really considered all the tasks involved can feel challenging.

Making a list of mini-tasks can also be an effective way to plan your day. Even if you don't think this will work for you, give it a try for a few days and see.

The evening before, make a list of all the tasks you need to do for the following day. This likely means a list of 50 or so items. This might very well be overkill, but try it anyway. You can always scale back as needed. If you often feel like you never get anything done, this might be a great tool to apply daily.

Mini-tasks are a viable way of completing large or complex projects.

By breaking everything down into simple, small, and manageable components, you're much less likely to procrastinate. For a lot of people, this is a very effective way to consistently get a lot done. Try mini-tasking instead of multi-tasking and watch your efficiency soar!

Do More in Less Time - And Have More Time for Yourself

Getting things done brings such a great feeling of accomplishment, but it can also be overwhelming if the task seems insurmountable. Sometimes, the days just don't seem long enough to do everything we want to do. When that happens, worry can set in, but it doesn't have to!

You can do more than you ever thought was possible, and in less time too, giving yourself time to relax and really enjoy life!

It all begins with a solid foundation of time management and scheduling. It's okay if you're not a good time manager right now, you can learn to be. It just takes a little bit of practice and you'll soon be getting more and more done.

When you see how much you're accomplishing, you'll work even harder during your busy times, and enjoy those down times more thoroughly.

These scheduling strategies will help you become an expert manager of your time:

1. Schedule your life for maximum benefit. You can avoid procrastination and the big stressed-out rush to meet a deadline by scheduling each day and using just a bit of self-discipline to stick to your schedule.

    - ***Mini-tasking!*** *(see previous page)*

    - By scheduling your day according to your priorities, you can better utilise the time that you might otherwise have wasted doing unproductive things, like watching television or waiting for the next item on your to-do list to come to you.

2. Disallow doubts from getting in your way. That little voice in the back of your mind that tells you, *"It's too much work,"* or *"It's not going to happen,"* doesn't know what it's talking about!

    - *You can do anything you set your mind to.* Keep that thought in mind as you go through your day. The more you think it - or even say it out loud - the more you'll internalise and believe it. (See your free Affirmation poster!)

    - When you remind yourself how much you're capable of doing, you'll work harder so you can reap the rewards of being done with work.

    - *No matter how you reward yourself, make it a point to do so regularly.* Finished that presentation? Take the evening off and watch your favourite movie!

Whatever reward works for you is a good one - as long as the work is done first.

3. Recognise when you're getting stressed and why. Sometimes, in an effort to get more done, you'll find that you aren't getting the time for yourself that you'd hoped for. When this happens, stop and reassess your schedule.

    - Are you following your agenda? Are you productive during your scheduled working times? Are you meeting your goals? Where can you make changes for better success?

    - Do you concentrate and get your work done during your working hours? If not, you may find that you still have to work when you should be relaxing. This is a vicious circle that leaves you feeling stressed, while getting nowhere.

4. Eliminate your stressors while building in stress relief. Think about the following as you go about your workday:

    - By focusing during working hours, you'll complete each task much sooner. Get your drudgery tasks out of the way as quickly as possible to make more time for more enjoyable tasks.

    - *Work time is for work only - so avoid distractions.* Ringing phones and other issues can stop you from accomplishing your work. Forward calls to your voice mail and establish "do not disturb" times. You'll be amazed at how much work you can get done without distractions!

    - If you complete your tasks early, keep working until your schedule says it's time to stop. Perhaps you can tackle some work for the next day to get ahead. Being a little ahead gives you the flexibility to take care of inevitable emergencies without falling behind in productivity.

    - *Recognise when you need a break.* People are not machines so your schedule should reflect that. Realistic break times should be part of even the busiest schedule.

By planning your time wisely, you'll accomplish more and be able to reap the many benefits of true relaxation when you're done. It's well worth the effort!

CHAPTER 4
Bookkeeping Your AVON Business

In this section, we'll be looking at how to bookkeep your business and I've also provided you with the tools to bookkeep your business within this book.

You would also find it useful to find a folder to keep all your Avon invoices and any other relevant paperwork.

Introduction to Bookkeeping Your Business

You'll be using a system of accounting known as cash accounting. This just means that you are accounting for a transaction on the date that money changes hands, not based on order dates. For example, a customer makes an order for £25 on 27th April, and you deliver it and receive the money on 7th May. You will account for that transaction on the 7th May, not the 27th April.

This might feel like a huge amount to take in, especially if you've never done anything beyond your own personal finances before, but take it slowly, ask questions where you need to and don't let it overwhelm you. You can do this!

Bank Account

If you can, get a bank account that is solely dedicated to your Avon business. It doesn't *have* to be a business bank account as this can often cost you more to run.

The idea behind this is that it will be easier to keep track of your Avon transactions, but also remind you to keep your Avon business finances separate from your personal finances. So, for example when you make a purchase of Avon product for your own personal use, you transfer the cost of that from your personal bank account to your Avon bank account.

There are loads of online banks that allow you to setup a bank account relatively easily, I've use many of them, of both business and personal accounts, but my favourite (for a personal account) is Monzo.

VIDEO – Click on Link **"4-1: Bank Account"**

Turnover, Sales, Cost of Sales, Business Expenses...aaahhh!!

There is a lot of terminology involved here, and it does help to have an understanding before continuing. I have simplified it in some areas, as you don't need to know the full accounting definitions in order to get the right numbers in the right places.

Sales/Turnover – you will see I use these words interchangeably. Basically, it is the amount of money that a business takes. With our Avon business, this would be:

- Customer orders – what the customer actually paid for their order (including any loyalty or Avon Angel discounts and freebie items etc. This means it's not necessarily what it says as book price on your Avon invoice (another reason why I advise that you keep your order forms!);
- Sales prices at Markets or Events;
- Commission received from direct delivery through your online store.

Cost of Sales – the cost of product needed to fulfil the orders that make up your turnover figure and any other costs your business needs your to spend to achieve those orders (brochures, demos, loyalty gifts etc).

Gross Profit is your turnover less your cost of sales. The self assessment tax return doesn't ask for this figure.

Expenses - the rest of your expenses are things like mileage, work from home, business cards, bank/cc processing costs, postage etc etc)

Net Profit is calculated as Turnover less Cost of Sales less Expenses. Or you can calculate it as Gross Profit less Expenses.
Again, not a figure that your tax return asks for, but does calculate it for you from the turnover and expense figures. It should match your net profit calculation, if it doesn't you'll need to figure out why. It is this figure that is taxed at the amount appropriate to your circumstances.

The **Trading Allowance** lets you take turnover of less than £1000 and apply the allowance to that turnover to make it a zero taxable amount. You cannot apply the trading allowance to a figure that has already had costs removed from it, which is why we look at turnover/sales.

VIDEO – Click on Link **"4-2: Terminology"**

Turnover/Sales

If you look at the first section on the campaign record sheet (starting on page 39), we start off looking at the sales and turnover

VIDEO – Click on Link **"4-3: Turnover/Sales"**

Orders and Sales to Customers

Keep all order forms from customers and a list of sales you make if you do a market stall/event.

Some people tell you that you don't need to keep order forms because the Avon invoice is enough. The problem is, your Avon invoice doesn't prove what was a sale to a customer, what was bought as stock or what was a personal purchase etc. Keeping your order forms means at least you can prove your sales. I usually write myself an order form for any personal purchases too.

Recording the information from your Avon Invoice

You will need: 5 different colour highlighters or pens; a calculator (or calculator app); pencil; some patience.

1. Create a key for your different coloured pens, it might look something like this:
    a. Green = Customer order
    b. Pink = Stock
    c. Yellow = Demos/Samples
    d. Blue = Sales tools
    e. Orange = Personal Purchases
    f. Purple = Returns to Avon
2. Go through your invoice and highlight every line based on what it is from the key.
3. Create a totals box at the bottom of your invoice; add up all your green lines and put the total in; then add up all your pink lines and put your total in etc. Do this part with a pencil so you can erase it if you get anything wrong.
4. Add up the 4 purchase totals and take away your returns figure – it should match the total figure payable on the invoice.

A couple of notes on the above:

- You are looking at **"Your cost"**, not "Brochure Price each", "Price total" or "Your discount" on the invoice. We are looking at what it costs your business to buy the product before you resell them.
- We'll look at returns again in the next section, as it seems to confuse a lot of people!

Returns to Customer

This part is frequently confused with returns to Avon – at this stage we are ONLY looking at what happens when a customer has paid for their item, and they want to return it. You have to refund the customer and remove the sale from your figures, so all you'll do is put what you returned to the customer into the right box as a negative.

Expenses

Let's look at expenses you can claim against your income:

Avon Expenses

Any product that fulfils a customer order, purchased as stock to sell online or at an event, purchased to give away to customers or your team as incentives, as demo for CUSTOMERS to try and any books/brochures and business items that you have purchased from Avon's business supplies are all valid business expenses.

You CANNOT claim for :
- Any product that you have purchased for yourself;
- Any product that you have purchased to demo ON YOURSELF
- Any product that you have purchased as gifts for family members or friends (birthday, Christmas etc).

Returns to Avon

This is where you put the amount that you get credited back from Avon into your numbers. Ultimately it will reduce your cost of sales.

VIDEO – Click on Link **"4-4: Avon Expenses and Returns"**

Mileage

You can claim mileage you drive for business reasons at 45p per mile (for cars and vans – it's different rate if you use a motor bike or bicycle). This covers both fuel and wear and tear on your vehicle, so **no** other motor costs should be claimed in addition to mileage.

Make sure you keep a record of the miles you drive - HMRC could ask to see your records at any time. Later in this book there is a mileage log, and if you need additional pages, there is a PDF of the same page available to download in the group.

If you are registered for VAT there is a clever little trick you can use to claim back a small portion of the VAT on the fuel element of the mileage allowance – have a look in the group for that as it's likely not relevant for most of you.

Note on VAT: You will know if you are registered for VAT – you have to actively do it through the HMRC website and you will be submitting VAT returns quarterly. You don't need to worry about becoming VAT registered until you reach about £85,000 in sales each year.

VIDEO – Click on Link **"4-5: Mileage"**

Other Travel Costs

If you had to take a train or bus to make your Avon deliveries, you can include the cost of the ticket in your expenses. Also if you had to pay for parking.

Working from Home

I recommend using the simplified expenses calculation for this, the link to the HMRC website explaining it can be found below, along with the video I've recorded to explain it.

The amount you claim is based on the number of hours you work per month.

There are a couple of other ways to calculate this, but one is much more involved, and the other isn't technically correct. I'm not going to go through these options here, if you'd like more info on these, they can be found in the Facebook Group.

VIDEO – Click on Link **"4-6: Working from Home Allowance"**

Other Sales Materials

Any stickers, business cards, leaflets, car decals etc that you have printed from a 3rd party supplier like Vista Print can all be included as expenses.

Telephone Costs

If you have a phone specifically for your AVON business you can include the costs in your expenses.

If you use your personal or home phone, any *direct* costs that you've incurred you can include here i.e anything that is separately identified and charged on your phone bill – you cannot just claim the entirety of your personal phone contract. And technically claiming a percentage of your personal contracts is also not technically correct (although some accountants do actually recommend this, so clearly it isn't enforced particularly strongly by HMRC – so it's up to you how you include this!).

If you can prove that you have upgraded to a more expensive contract so you can run your business, you could claim the difference.

Broadband/Internet Costs

You'll need to find a reasonable method of dividing your costs, eg by the number of rooms you use for business or the amount of time you spend working from home. (They won't accept that you are working 100% of the time, so be reasonable!).

For example, if you are working 3 hours per day only while the children are at school, with 20 working days per month (on average) you are looking at 60 working hours per month. As a percentage of total hours per month (30 times 24 = 720), you'll find 60/720 = 0.08 = 8%. If your broadband fee is £25 per month, you'll be able to claim £2 per month.

Printer Costs

If you've printed anything with your home printer, you can include any ink or paper costs. Don't include the full costs of those things if you use the printer for anything not related to Avon – eg the children's homework!

Clothing

If you buy any Avon *branded* clothing or clothing you've had printed/embroidered that you use for promotional purposes i.e "Ask me for an Avon brochure", you can claim the costs. Don't try to claim anything like rain jacket or walking shoes – there really is no way you can prove that they are not being used for personal use.

Bank/Merchant Costs

If you have a bank account that you use purely for Avon, you can claim any costs associated with running the account. Also, any merchant fees you incur processing payments from customers through processors such as PayPal, Stripe, Sumup, Square etc

Marketing/Advertising

If you have spent any money advertising (eg Facebook boost) or building/hosting a website, then you can include them as valid business expenses. Also include any costs of a stand or exhibition fee if you have a stand selling Avon product.

Accountancy/Professional Costs

If you pay an accountant to do your return for you, or if you pay for any bookkeeping software etc, then you can include all those costs. Oh, and the cost of this book is also a valid business expense!

CHAPTER 5
Submitting Your Tax Return

Submitting your tax return isn't as scary as you think. Just follow the instructions and do the best you can. As long as you have done everything in good faith and to the best of your ability, you are unlikely to be penalised if you have done anything wrong. The problem comes when you are seen to be deliberately manipulating your numbers so that you pay less tax.

Logging In

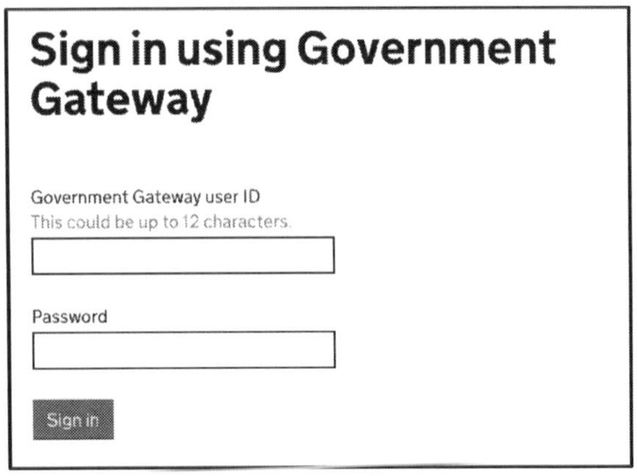

Sign in using Government Gateway
Government Gateway user ID
This could be up to 12 characters.
Password
Sign in

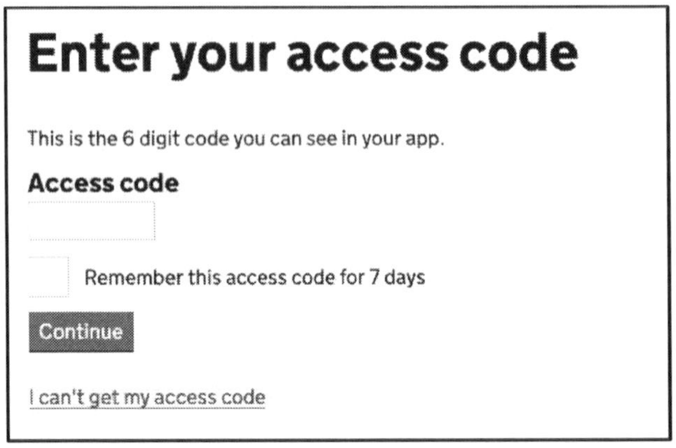

Enter your access code
This is the 6 digit code you can see in your app.
Access code
Remember this access code for 7 days
Continue
I can't get my access code

When you've logged in to your account, you'll see something like the screen below. You'll need to click on the Self-Assessment link on the right-hand side.

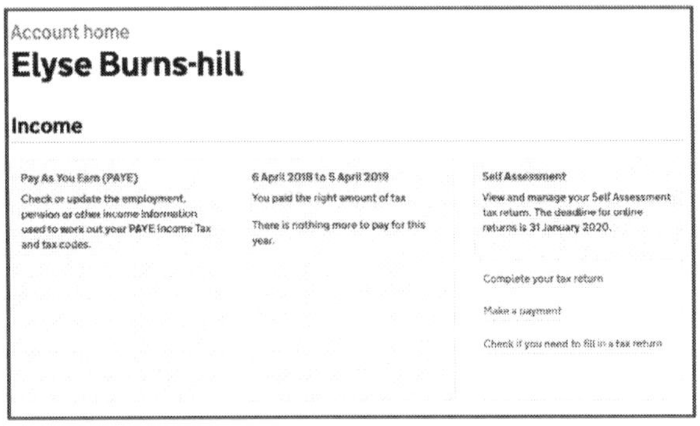

Account home
Elyse Burns-hill
Income
Pay As You Earn (PAYE)
Check or update the employment, pension or other income information used to work out your PAYE Income Tax and tax codes.
6 April 2018 to 5 April 2019
You paid the right amount of tax
There is nothing more to pay for this year.
Self Assessment
View and manage your Self Assessment tax return. The deadline for online returns is 31 January 2020.
Complete your tax return
Make a payment
Check if you need to fill in a tax return

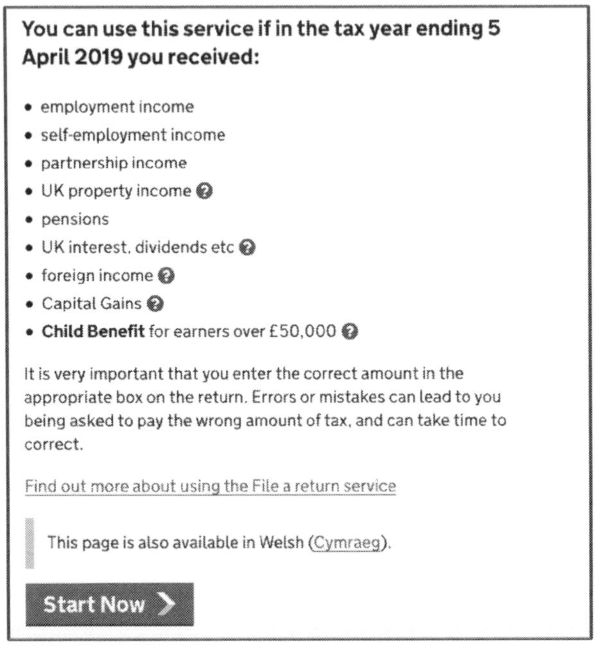

You can use this service if in the tax year ending 5 April 2019 you received:
employment income
self-employment income
partnership income
UK property income
pensions
UK interest, dividends etc
foreign income
Capital Gains
Child Benefit for earners over £50,000
It is very important that you enter the correct amount in the appropriate box on the return. Errors or mistakes can lead to you being asked to pay the wrong amount of tax, and can take time to correct.
Find out more about using the File a return service
This page is also available in Welsh (Cymraeg).
Start Now

You will be then asked to check that you should be using this service – and as you have self-employment income, you will, so click on start.

If you have any problems logging on, your best bet is to give the tax office a ring. You might also need passport or P60 to be able to log on – I think if you haven't setup an access code (using either your mobile phone number or the HMRC app) then it asks for other forms of ID when logging in.

Tailoring Your Return

Once you're into your return, if will ask for some information about you. I won't go through the answers for this, because hopefully you'll know the answers to these questions!

The next stage is to start tailoring your return. You can come back and change this at any time before you submit your return. So, if you complete it and then realise your return hasn't asked you about something, then you'll need to come back and review your answers to the tailoring questions.

Page 1

It asks you about whether you were an employee, whether your turnover was more than £1000 and how many self-employments you had, whether you received any money from UK property or land, foreign earnings and whether you had any chargeable gains from disposal of assets.

Just to be clear, you are employed if you work for someone else and receive a payslip which shows PAYE, national insurance and possibly pension lines. As an employee you will receive a P60 form from your employer, which you will need to complete your tax return.

The chargeable gains section is asking about disposal of large assets where it has increased in value, for example a house or property, maybe a family heirloom. If you might have something like this, I'd recommend getting an appointment with an Accountant as you'll want to make sure you're treating it correctly.

VIDEO – Click on Link **"5-1: Tailor your return 1"**

Page 2

In this section you'll be asked about:

- interest income (e.g from your bank accounts – you'll know if you did, you'll just need to review bank statements to find out exactly how much);
- dividend income (you'll know if you did – you'll be holding investments or you'll be a shareholder of a company);
- UK pensions, annuities or state benefits (state pension, occupational pension, retirement annuity, incapacity benefit etc);
- whether you were entitled to receive child benefit, and whether your personal income was over £50,000;
- whether you received any other UK income eg employment sums, share schemes or life insurance gains;
- whether you made and tax losses in the year (eg with your Avon Business);
- pension savings tax charges (you'll know what this is if it applies).

VIDEO – Click on Link **"5-2: Tailor your return 2"**

Page 3

In the last page of tailoring questions, it asks about:

- whether you made contributions to a personal pension or retirement annuity (not including payments that went through your payslip to your employer's pension scheme as this has already been dealt with correctly);
- whether you gave any money to charity (specifically thinking about whether you said yes to gift aid at any point during the year;
- whether you want to claim married couple's allowance IF you were born before 6 April 1935;
- whether you want to transfer 10% of your personal allowance to your spouse or civil partner (if you earn below the tax threshold - £12,500 for 19/20 tax year – but your spouse earns over the personal allowance, you can transfer up to 10% of your personal allowance, so that he/she has a larger personal allowance before tax kicks in, which at 20% can mean a £250 saving), make sure you understand what you are doing here before you click yes;
- whether you want to claim any other tax reliefs and deductions – you'll probably know if you've done something in the year that this applies to, so if you don't, just click no;
- whether you've had any 19/20 tax refunded or offset by HMRC or the Job Centre. You will have received notification if this is the case;
- "Did you have a tax adviser" – I am not your adviser and this book does not serve as advice – if anything I consider myself to be a translator (from HMRC gobbledygook to English!). Please see the disclaimer at the front of the book! If you did use a tax adviser then click yes, if you didn't click no;

- whether you used a tax avoidance scheme. There is a difference between tax avoidance and tax evasion – tax evasion is illegal and can be done by not declaring income and not paying tax when you should have done. Tax avoidance is not illegal but is generally quite an aggressive interpretation of the tax law – what the big companies like Costa, Apple and Google do could be tax avoidance. It goes beyond simple tax planning, so I expect your answer will probably be no to this one;
- Disguised remuneration avoidance schemes would relate to the issue that's been in the news recently about all these umbrella schemes that people used to pay themselves. Hopefully you'll know if this applies to you;
- The final question is about whether you are completing the return yourself – the answer is probably yes!

VIDEO – Click on Link **"5-3: Tailor your return 3"**

Fill in your Return

First page, you'll see what documentation you'll need to complete your return. Obviously, you won't necessarily need all of it, when you have finished tailoring your return, you'll be told exactly what you need.

> **Fill in your return**
>
> Check your progress
>
> To complete your return you may need the following documents:
>
> - P60 or P45 (Part 1A)
> - P11D or equivalent information from your employer
> - Profit or loss accounts
> - Records of business receipts and business expenses
> - Bank statements or any receipts from the charity
> - 2018 to 2019 and 2019 to 2020 Notices of Coding
>
> This section provides you with an overview of what pages make up your tailored return.
> ✔ A tick means you have entered information into this page. To change this please select from the list below.
> ✚ A plus means you have yet to enter information into this page.

VIDEO – Click on Link **"5-4: Fill in your Return 1"**

The next section is about employment details – so this will be about any employments that you had during the tax year. If it doesn't show up, and you were employed, you'll need to go back and adjust your answers in the tailoring section.

VIDEO – Click on Link **"5-5: Fill in your Return 2"**

Next comes your self-employment – either just your Avon Business or other self-employed businesses if that applies to you.

VIDEO – Click on Link **“5-6: Fill in your Return 3”**

National Insurance Class 2 is payable if you earn over a certain amount, so this section will take you through if you have to pay any or if you want to voluntarily pay any.

VIDEO – Click on Link **“5-7: Fill in your Return 4”**

If you said you’d given to charity in your tailoring section, this will ask you more detail.

VIDEO – Click on Link **“5-8: Fill in your Return 5”**

The penultimate page asks you information about your tax coding and whether you’ve over/underpaid tax through your coding.

VIDEO – Click on Link **“5-9: Fill in your Return 6”**

The final page is asking you to check your return and shows you all the calculations.

VIDEO – Click on Link **“5-10: Fill in your Return 7”**

CHAPTER 6
Bookkeeping Sheets

Over the rest of this chapter you will find the sheets you'll need to record all your financial information that you will need to be able to submit your Self-Assessment Tax Return.

Summary Sheet

This sheet asks for the totals from each of the Campaign Sheets and then shows you how to total the numbers up

Here are the formulas you need to be able to complete the Summary Sheet:

Q	=	L						
R	=	M	+	N	+	O	+	P
S	=	Q	-	R				
T	=	S	x	your tax rate				

Campaign Sheets

There are 20 of these pages, so with only 18 campaigns, it should mean you have a couple left over. Each Campaign Sheet has 5 order columns on it so that you can separate out your different orders. Follow the descriptions on the left and complete the boxes on the right. At the bottom of the sheet, you have a Campaign Summary section – it is these numbers you will need to copy across to the Summary Sheet.

Here are the formulas you will need to complete the Campaign Sheets:

F	=	A	+	A	+	A	+	A	-	B	+	A
G	=	C	+	C	+	C	+	C	-	D		
H	=	F	-	G								
I	=	Total of E's										
J	=	F	+	F								
K	=	H	-	I	-	J						

Mileage Log and Timesheet

I've included a mileage log and timesheet so you have somewhere safe to keep your notes on where you've driven and how long you've spent working on your business so that you can calculate your mileage and working from home allowances.

Income/Expenses Statement

Campaign Totals

	Sales	Cost of Sales	Admin Exp	Finance Exp	Net Profit
Campaign ________					
Campaign ________					
Campaign ________					
Campaign ________					
Campaign ________					
Campaign ________					
Campaign ________					
Campaign ________					
Campaign ________					
Campaign ________					
Campaign ________					
Campaign ________					
Campaign ________					
Campaign ________					
Campaign ________					
Campaign ________					
Campaign ________					
Campaign ________					
Campaign ________					
Campaign ________					
TOTAL					
	L	M	N	O	

Working from Home Allowance

Hours		0-24	25-50	51-100	101+
Flat Rate to claim		0.00	10.00	18.00	26.00

	No of hours	Flate rate
Example	34.00	10.00
April		
May		
June		
July		
August		
September		
October		
November		
December		
January		
February		
March		
TOTAL		
		P

Summary

Total Sales	L	Q
Total Expenses	M + N + O + P	R
Profit	Q - R	S
Expected Tax	S x 20%	

Campaign ________

Income/Expenses Statement	Order 1	Order 2	Order 3	Order 4	Order 5	Camp Total	
Turnover/Sales							
Sales Value of Customer Orders							A
Sales Value of Market/Event Purchases							A
Sales Value of Ebay/Facebook Purchases							A
Commission received from online sales							A
Value of returns you gave back to Customer							B
Sales Leader Commission & Rewards							A
Cost of Sales (Avon Invoice)							
Cost of Customer Purchases this month							C
Cost of Stock Items purchased this month							C
Cost of Demos/Samples purchased this month							C
Cost of Sales tools purchased this month							C
Credit of returns on this invoice							D
Business related costs							
Number of miles driven in car							
Miles x 0.45							E
Other Travel costs							E
Purchase of other sales materials							E
Telephone costs							E
Internet/broadband costs							E
Printer costs							E
Clothing							E
Marketing/Advertising							E
Postage							E
Accountancy and professional costs							E
Bank costs/processing fees							F
Avon direct delivery fees							F

Campaign Summary

	Order 1 £	Order 2 £	Order 3 £	Order 4 £	Order 5 £	**This Camp £**	
Turnover/Sales							F
Cost of Sales							G
Gross Profit/(Loss)							H
Administrative Expenses							I
Financial Expenses							J
Net Profit							K

Campaign ________

Income/Expenses Statement	Order 1	Order 2	Order 3	Order 4	Order 5	Camp Total	
Turnover/Sales							
Sales Value of Customer Orders							A
Sales Value of Market/Event Purchases							A
Sales Value of Ebay/Facebook Purchases							A
Commission received from online sales							A
Value of returns you gave back to Customer							B
Sales Leader Commission & Rewards							A
Cost of Sales (Avon Invoice)							
Cost of Customer Purchases this month							C
Cost of Stock Items purchased this month							C
Cost of Demos/Samples purchased this month							C
Cost of Sales tools purchased this month							C
Credit of returns on this invoice							D
Business related costs							
Number of miles driven in car							
Miles x 0.45							E
Other Travel costs							E
Purchase of other sales materials							E
Telephone costs							E
Internet/broadband costs							E
Printer costs							E
Clothing							E
Marketing/Advertising							E
Postage							E
Accountancy and professional costs							E
Bank costs/processing fees							F
Avon direct delivery fees							F

Campaign Summary

	Order 1 £	Order 2 £	Order 3 £	Order 4 £	Order 5 £	**This Camp £**	
Turnover/Sales							F
Cost of Sales							G
Gross Profit/(Loss)							H
Administrative Expenses							I
Financial Expenses							J
Net Profit							K

Campaign ________

Income/Expenses Statement	Order 1	Order 2	Order 3	Order 4	Order 5	Camp Total	
Turnover/Sales							
Sales Value of Customer Orders							A
Sales Value of Market/Event Purchases							A
Sales Value of Ebay/Facebook Purchases							A
Commission received from online sales							A
Value of returns you gave back to Customer							B
Sales Leader Commission & Rewards							A
Cost of Sales (Avon Invoice)							
Cost of Customer Purchases this month							C
Cost of Stock Items purchased this month							C
Cost of Demos/Samples purchased this month							C
Cost of Sales tools purchased this month							C
Credit of returns on this invoice							D
Business related costs							
Number of miles driven in car							
Miles x 0.45							E
Other Travel costs							E
Purchase of other sales materials							E
Telephone costs							E
Internet/broadband costs							E
Printer costs							E
Clothing							E
Marketing/Advertising							E
Postage							E
Accountancy and professional costs							E
Bank costs/processing fees							F
Avon direct delivery fees							F

Campaign Summary

	Order 1 £	Order 2 £	Order 3 £	Order 4 £	Order 5 £	**This Camp £**	
Turnover/Sales							F
Cost of Sales							G
Gross Profit/(Loss)							H
Administrative Expenses							I
Financial Expenses							J
Net Profit							K

Campaign ________

Income/Expenses Statement	**Order 1**	**Order 2**	**Order 3**	**Order 4**	**Order 5**	**Camp Total**	
Turnover/Sales							
Sales Value of Customer Orders							A
Sales Value of Market/Event Purchases							A
Sales Value of Ebay/Facebook Purchases							A
Commission received from online sales							A
Value of returns you gave back to Customer							B
Sales Leader Commission & Rewards							A
Cost of Sales (Avon Invoice)							
Cost of Customer Purchases this month							C
Cost of Stock Items purchased this month							C
Cost of Demos/Samples purchased this month							C
Cost of Sales tools purchased this month							C
Credit of returns on this invoice							D
Business related costs							
Number of miles driven in car							
Miles x 0.45							E
Other Travel costs							E
Purchase of other sales materials							E
Telephone costs							E
Internet/broadband costs							E
Printer costs							E
Clothing							E
Marketing/Advertising							E
Postage							E
Accountancy and professional costs							E
Bank costs/processing fees							F
Avon direct delivery fees							F

Campaign Summary

	Order 1 £	Order 2 £	Order 3 £	Order 4 £	Order 5 £	**This Camp £**	
Turnover/Sales							F
Cost of Sales							G
Gross Profit/(Loss)							H
Administrative Expenses							I
Financial Expenses							J
Net Profit							K

Campaign ________

Income/Expenses Statement	Order 1	Order 2	Order 3	Order 4	Order 5	Camp Total	
Turnover/Sales							
Sales Value of Customer Orders							A
Sales Value of Market/Event Purchases							A
Sales Value of Ebay/Facebook Purchases							A
Commission received from online sales							A
Value of returns you gave back to Customer							B
Sales Leader Commission & Rewards							A
Cost of Sales (Avon Invoice)							
Cost of Customer Purchases this month							C
Cost of Stock Items purchased this month							C
Cost of Demos/Samples purchased this month							C
Cost of Sales tools purchased this month							C
Credit of returns on this invoice							D
Business related costs							
Number of miles driven in car							
Miles x 0.45							E
Other Travel costs							E
Purchase of other sales materials							E
Telephone costs							E
Internet/broadband costs							E
Printer costs							E
Clothing							E
Marketing/Advertising							E
Postage							E
Accountancy and professional costs							E
Bank costs/processing fees							F
Avon direct delivery fees							F

Campaign Summary

	Order 1 £	Order 2 £	Order 3 £	Order 4 £	Order 5 £	**This Camp £**	
Turnover/Sales							F
Cost of Sales							G
Gross Profit/(Loss)							H
Administrative Expenses							I
Financial Expenses							J
Net Profit							K

Campaign ________

Income/Expenses Statement	Order 1	Order 2	Order 3	Order 4	Order 5	Camp Total	
Turnover/Sales							
Sales Value of Customer Orders							A
Sales Value of Market/Event Purchases							A
Sales Value of Ebay/Facebook Purchases							A
Commission received from online sales							A
Value of returns you gave back to Customer							B
Sales Leader Commission & Rewards							A
Cost of Sales (Avon Invoice)							
Cost of Customer Purchases this month							C
Cost of Stock Items purchased this month							C
Cost of Demos/Samples purchased this month							C
Cost of Sales tools purchased this month							C
Credit of returns on this invoice							D
Business related costs							
Number of miles driven in car							
Miles x 0.45							E
Other Travel costs							E
Purchase of other sales materials							E
Telephone costs							E
Internet/broadband costs							E
Printer costs							E
Clothing							E
Marketing/Advertising							E
Postage							E
Accountancy and professional costs							E
Bank costs/processing fees							F
Avon direct delivery fees							F

Campaign Summary

	Order 1 £	Order 2 £	Order 3 £	Order 4 £	Order 5 £	**This Camp £**	
Turnover/Sales							F
Cost of Sales							G
Gross Profit/(Loss)							H
Administrative Expenses							I
Financial Expenses							J
Net Profit							K

Campaign ________

Income/Expenses Statement	Order 1	Order 2	Order 3	Order 4	Order 5	Camp Total	
Turnover/Sales							
Sales Value of Customer Orders							A
Sales Value of Market/Event Purchases							A
Sales Value of Ebay/Facebook Purchases							A
Commission received from online sales							A
Value of returns you gave back to Customer							B
Sales Leader Commission & Rewards							A
Cost of Sales (Avon Invoice)							
Cost of Customer Purchases this month							C
Cost of Stock Items purchased this month							C
Cost of Demos/Samples purchased this month							C
Cost of Sales tools purchased this month							C
Credit of returns on this invoice							D
Business related costs							
Number of miles driven in car							
Miles x 0.45							E
Other Travel costs							E
Purchase of other sales materials							E
Telephone costs							E
Internet/broadband costs							E
Printer costs							E
Clothing							E
Marketing/Advertising							E
Postage							E
Accountancy and professional costs							E
Bank costs/processing fees							F
Avon direct delivery fees							F

Campaign Summary

	Order 1 £	Order 2 £	Order 3 £	Order 4 £	Order 5 £	**This Camp £**	
Turnover/Sales							F
Cost of Sales							G
Gross Profit/(Loss)							H
Administrative Expenses							I
Financial Expenses							J
Net Profit							K

Campaign ________

Income/Expenses Statement	Order 1	Order 2	Order 3	Order 4	Order 5	Camp Total	
Turnover/Sales							
Sales Value of Customer Orders							A
Sales Value of Market/Event Purchases							A
Sales Value of Ebay/Facebook Purchases							A
Commission received from online sales							A
Value of returns you gave back to Customer							B
Sales Leader Commission & Rewards							A
Cost of Sales (Avon Invoice)							
Cost of Customer Purchases this month							C
Cost of Stock Items purchased this month							C
Cost of Demos/Samples purchased this month							C
Cost of Sales tools purchased this month							C
Credit of returns on this invoice							D
Business related costs							
Number of miles driven in car							
Miles x 0.45							E
Other Travel costs							E
Purchase of other sales materials							E
Telephone costs							E
Internet/broadband costs							E
Printer costs							E
Clothing							E
Marketing/Advertising							E
Postage							E
Accountancy and professional costs							E
Bank costs/processing fees							F
Avon direct delivery fees							F

Campaign Summary

	Order 1 £	Order 2 £	Order 3 £	Order 4 £	Order 5 £	**This Camp £**	
Turnover/Sales							F
Cost of Sales							G
Gross Profit/(Loss)							H
Administrative Expenses							I
Financial Expenses							J
Net Profit							K

Campaign ________

Income/Expenses Statement	Order 1	Order 2	Order 3	Order 4	Order 5	Camp Total	
Turnover/Sales							
Sales Value of Customer Orders							A
Sales Value of Market/Event Purchases							A
Sales Value of Ebay/Facebook Purchases							A
Commission received from online sales							A
Value of returns you gave back to Customer							B
Sales Leader Commission & Rewards							A
Cost of Sales (Avon Invoice)							
Cost of Customer Purchases this month							C
Cost of Stock Items purchased this month							C
Cost of Demos/Samples purchased this month							C
Cost of Sales tools purchased this month							C
Credit of returns on this invoice							D
Business related costs							
Number of miles driven in car							
Miles x 0.45							E
Other Travel costs							E
Purchase of other sales materials							E
Telephone costs							E
Internet/broadband costs							E
Printer costs							E
Clothing							E
Marketing/Advertising							E
Postage							E
Accountancy and professional costs							E
Bank costs/processing fees							F
Avon direct delivery fees							F

Campaign Summary

	Order 1 £	Order 2 £	Order 3 £	Order 4 £	Order 5 £	**This Camp £**	
Turnover/Sales							F
Cost of Sales							G
Gross Profit/(Loss)							H
Administrative Expenses							I
Financial Expenses							J
Net Profit							K

Campaign ________

Income/Expenses Statement	Order 1	Order 2	Order 3	Order 4	Order 5	Camp Total	
Turnover/Sales							
Sales Value of Customer Orders							A
Sales Value of Market/Event Purchases							A
Sales Value of Ebay/Facebook Purchases							A
Commission received from online sales							A
Value of returns you gave back to Customer							B
Sales Leader Commission & Rewards							A
Cost of Sales (Avon Invoice)							
Cost of Customer Purchases this month							C
Cost of Stock Items purchased this month							C
Cost of Demos/Samples purchased this month							C
Cost of Sales tools purchased this month							C
Credit of returns on this invoice							D
Business related costs							
Number of miles driven in car							
Miles x 0.45							E
Other Travel costs							E
Purchase of other sales materials							E
Telephone costs							E
Internet/broadband costs							E
Printer costs							E
Clothing							E
Marketing/Advertising							E
Postage							E
Accountancy and professional costs							E
Bank costs/processing fees							F
Avon direct delivery fees							F

Campaign Summary

	Order 1 £	Order 2 £	Order 3 £	Order 4 £	Order 5 £	**This Camp** **£**	
Turnover/Sales							F
Cost of Sales							G
Gross Profit/(Loss)							H
Administrative Expenses							I
Financial Expenses							J
Net Profit							K

Campaign ________

Income/Expenses Statement	Order 1	Order 2	Order 3	Order 4	Order 5	Camp Total	
Turnover/Sales							
Sales Value of Customer Orders							A
Sales Value of Market/Event Purchases							A
Sales Value of Ebay/Facebook Purchases							A
Commission received from online sales							A
Value of returns you gave back to Customer							B
Sales Leader Commission & Rewards							A
Cost of Sales (Avon Invoice)							
Cost of Customer Purchases this month							C
Cost of Stock Items purchased this month							C
Cost of Demos/Samples purchased this month							C
Cost of Sales tools purchased this month							C
Credit of returns on this invoice							D
Business related costs							
Number of miles driven in car							
Miles x 0.45							E
Other Travel costs							E
Purchase of other sales materials							E
Telephone costs							E
Internet/broadband costs							E
Printer costs							E
Clothing							E
Marketing/Advertising							E
Postage							E
Accountancy and professional costs							E
Bank costs/processing fees							F
Avon direct delivery fees							F

Campaign Summary

	Order 1 £	Order 2 £	Order 3 £	Order 4 £	Order 5 £	**This Camp £**	
Turnover/Sales							F
Cost of Sales							G
Gross Profit/(Loss)							H
Administrative Expenses							I
Financial Expenses							J
Net Profit							K

Campaign ________

Income/Expenses Statement	Order 1	Order 2	Order 3	Order 4	Order 5	Camp Total	
Turnover/Sales							
Sales Value of Customer Orders							A
Sales Value of Market/Event Purchases							A
Sales Value of Ebay/Facebook Purchases							A
Commission received from online sales							A
Value of returns you gave back to Customer							B
Sales Leader Commission & Rewards							A
Cost of Sales (Avon Invoice)							
Cost of Customer Purchases this month							C
Cost of Stock Items purchased this month							C
Cost of Demos/Samples purchased this month							C
Cost of Sales tools purchased this month							C
Credit of returns on this invoice							D
Business related costs							
Number of miles driven in car							
Miles x 0.45							E
Other Travel costs							E
Purchase of other sales materials							E
Telephone costs							E
Internet/broadband costs							E
Printer costs							E
Clothing							E
Marketing/Advertising							E
Postage							E
Accountancy and professional costs							E
Bank costs/processing fees							F
Avon direct delivery fees							F

Campaign Summary

	Order 1 £	Order 2 £	Order 3 £	Order 4 £	Order 5 £	**This Camp £**	
Turnover/Sales							F
Cost of Sales							G
Gross Profit/(Loss)							H
Administrative Expenses							I
Financial Expenses							J
Net Profit							K

Campaign ________

Income/Expenses Statement	Order 1	Order 2	Order 3	Order 4	Order 5	Camp Total	
Turnover/Sales							
Sales Value of Customer Orders							A
Sales Value of Market/Event Purchases							A
Sales Value of Ebay/Facebook Purchases							A
Commission received from online sales							A
Value of returns you gave back to Customer							B
Sales Leader Commission & Rewards							A
Cost of Sales (Avon Invoice)							
Cost of Customer Purchases this month							C
Cost of Stock Items purchased this month							C
Cost of Demos/Samples purchased this month							C
Cost of Sales tools purchased this month							C
Credit of returns on this invoice							D
Business related costs							
Number of miles driven in car							
Miles x 0.45							E
Other Travel costs							E
Purchase of other sales materials							E
Telephone costs							E
Internet/broadband costs							E
Printer costs							E
Clothing							E
Marketing/Advertising							E
Postage							E
Accountancy and professional costs							E
Bank costs/processing fees							F
Avon direct delivery fees							F

Campaign Summary

	Order 1 £	Order 2 £	Order 3 £	Order 4 £	Order 5 £	**This Camp £**	
Turnover/Sales							F
Cost of Sales							G
Gross Profit/(Loss)							H
Administrative Expenses							I
Financial Expenses							J
Net Profit							K

Campaign ________

Income/Expenses Statement	Order 1	Order 2	Order 3	Order 4	Order 5	Camp Total	
Turnover/Sales							
Sales Value of Customer Orders							A
Sales Value of Market/Event Purchases							A
Sales Value of Ebay/Facebook Purchases							A
Commission received from online sales							A
Value of returns you gave back to Customer							B
Sales Leader Commission & Rewards							A
Cost of Sales (Avon Invoice)							
Cost of Customer Purchases this month							C
Cost of Stock Items purchased this month							C
Cost of Demos/Samples purchased this month							C
Cost of Sales tools purchased this month							C
Credit of returns on this invoice							D
Business related costs							
Number of miles driven in car							
Miles x 0.45							E
Other Travel costs							E
Purchase of other sales materials							E
Telephone costs							E
Internet/broadband costs							E
Printer costs							E
Clothing							E
Marketing/Advertising							E
Postage							E
Accountancy and professional costs							E
Bank costs/processing fees							F
Avon direct delivery fees							F

Campaign Summary

	Order 1 £	Order 2 £	Order 3 £	Order 4 £	Order 5 £	**This Camp £**	
Turnover/Sales							F
Cost of Sales							G
Gross Profit/(Loss)							H
Administrative Expenses							I
Financial Expenses							J
Net Profit							K

Campaign ________

Income/Expenses Statement	Order 1	Order 2	Order 3	Order 4	Order 5	Camp Total	
Turnover/Sales							
Sales Value of Customer Orders							A
Sales Value of Market/Event Purchases							A
Sales Value of Ebay/Facebook Purchases							A
Commission received from online sales							A
Value of returns you gave back to Customer							B
Sales Leader Commission & Rewards							A
Cost of Sales (Avon Invoice)							
Cost of Customer Purchases this month							C
Cost of Stock Items purchased this month							C
Cost of Demos/Samples purchased this month							C
Cost of Sales tools purchased this month							C
Credit of returns on this invoice							D
Business related costs							
Number of miles driven in car							
Miles x 0.45							E
Other Travel costs							E
Purchase of other sales materials							E
Telephone costs							E
Internet/broadband costs							E
Printer costs							E
Clothing							E
Marketing/Advertising							E
Postage							E
Accountancy and professional costs							E
Bank costs/processing fees							F
Avon direct delivery fees							F

Campaign Summary

	Order 1 £	Order 2 £	Order 3 £	Order 4 £	Order 5 £	**This Camp £**	
Turnover/Sales							F
Cost of Sales							G
Gross Profit/(Loss)							H
Administrative Expenses							I
Financial Expenses							J
Net Profit							K

Campaign ________

Income/Expenses Statement	Order 1	Order 2	Order 3	Order 4	Order 5	Camp Total	
Turnover/Sales							
Sales Value of Customer Orders							A
Sales Value of Market/Event Purchases							A
Sales Value of Ebay/Facebook Purchases							A
Commission received from online sales							A
Value of returns you gave back to Customer							B
Sales Leader Commission & Rewards							A
Cost of Sales (Avon Invoice)							
Cost of Customer Purchases this month							C
Cost of Stock Items purchased this month							C
Cost of Demos/Samples purchased this month							C
Cost of Sales tools purchased this month							C
Credit of returns on this invoice							D
Business related costs							
Number of miles driven in car							
Miles x 0.45							E
Other Travel costs							E
Purchase of other sales materials							E
Telephone costs							E
Internet/broadband costs							E
Printer costs							E
Clothing							E
Marketing/Advertising							E
Postage							E
Accountancy and professional costs							E
Bank costs/processing fees							F
Avon direct delivery fees							F

Campaign Summary

	Order 1 £	Order 2 £	Order 3 £	Order 4 £	Order 5 £	**This Camp** **£**	
Turnover/Sales							F
Cost of Sales							G
Gross Profit/(Loss)							H
Administrative Expenses							I
Financial Expenses							J
Net Profit							K

Campaign ________

Income/Expenses Statement	Order 1	Order 2	Order 3	Order 4	Order 5	Camp Total	
Turnover/Sales							
Sales Value of Customer Orders							A
Sales Value of Market/Event Purchases							A
Sales Value of Ebay/Facebook Purchases							A
Commission received from online sales							A
Value of returns you gave back to Customer							B
Sales Leader Commission & Rewards							A
Cost of Sales (Avon Invoice)							
Cost of Customer Purchases this month							C
Cost of Stock Items purchased this month							C
Cost of Demos/Samples purchased this month							C
Cost of Sales tools purchased this month							C
Credit of returns on this invoice							D
Business related costs							
Number of miles driven in car							
Miles x 0.45							E
Other Travel costs							E
Purchase of other sales materials							E
Telephone costs							E
Internet/broadband costs							E
Printer costs							E
Clothing							E
Marketing/Advertising							E
Postage							E
Accountancy and professional costs							E
Bank costs/processing fees							F
Avon direct delivery fees							F

Campaign Summary

	Order 1 £	Order 2 £	Order 3 £	Order 4 £	Order 5 £	**This Camp £**	
Turnover/Sales							F
Cost of Sales							G
Gross Profit/(Loss)							H
Administrative Expenses							I
Financial Expenses							J
Net Profit							K

Campaign ________

Income/Expenses Statement	Order 1	Order 2	Order 3	Order 4	Order 5	Camp Total	
Turnover/Sales							
Sales Value of Customer Orders							A
Sales Value of Market/Event Purchases							A
Sales Value of Ebay/Facebook Purchases							A
Commission received from online sales							A
Value of returns you gave back to Customer							B
Sales Leader Commission & Rewards							A
Cost of Sales (Avon Invoice)							
Cost of Customer Purchases this month							C
Cost of Stock Items purchased this month							C
Cost of Demos/Samples purchased this month							C
Cost of Sales tools purchased this month							C
Credit of returns on this invoice							D
Business related costs							
Number of miles driven in car							
Miles x 0.45							E
Other Travel costs							E
Purchase of other sales materials							E
Telephone costs							E
Internet/broadband costs							E
Printer costs							E
Clothing							E
Marketing/Advertising							E
Postage							E
Accountancy and professional costs							E
Bank costs/processing fees							F
Avon direct delivery fees							F

Campaign Summary

	Order 1 £	Order 2 £	Order 3 £	Order 4 £	Order 5 £	**This Camp £**	
Turnover/Sales							F
Cost of Sales							G
Gross Profit/(Loss)							H
Administrative Expenses							I
Financial Expenses							J
Net Profit							K

Campaign ________

Income/Expenses Statement	Order 1	Order 2	Order 3	Order 4	Order 5	Camp Total	
Turnover/Sales							
Sales Value of Customer Orders							A
Sales Value of Market/Event Purchases							A
Sales Value of Ebay/Facebook Purchases							A
Commission received from online sales							A
Value of returns you gave back to Customer							B
Sales Leader Commission & Rewards							A
Cost of Sales (Avon Invoice)							
Cost of Customer Purchases this month							C
Cost of Stock Items purchased this month							C
Cost of Demos/Samples purchased this month							C
Cost of Sales tools purchased this month							C
Credit of returns on this invoice							D
Business related costs							
Number of miles driven in car							
Miles x 0.45							E
Other Travel costs							E
Purchase of other sales materials							E
Telephone costs							E
Internet/broadband costs							E
Printer costs							E
Clothing							E
Marketing/Advertising							E
Postage							E
Accountancy and professional costs							E
Bank costs/processing fees							F
Avon direct delivery fees							F

Campaign Summary

	Order 1 £	Order 2 £	Order 3 £	Order 4 £	Order 5 £	**This Camp £**	
Turnover/Sales							F
Cost of Sales							G
Gross Profit/(Loss)							H
Administrative Expenses							I
Financial Expenses							J
Net Profit							K

Campaign ________

Income/Expenses Statement	Order 1	Order 2	Order 3	Order 4	Order 5	Camp Total	
Turnover/Sales							
Sales Value of Customer Orders							A
Sales Value of Market/Event Purchases							A
Sales Value of Ebay/Facebook Purchases							A
Commission received from online sales							A
Value of returns you gave back to Customer							B
Sales Leader Commission & Rewards							A
Cost of Sales (Avon Invoice)							
Cost of Customer Purchases this month							C
Cost of Stock Items purchased this month							C
Cost of Demos/Samples purchased this month							C
Cost of Sales tools purchased this month							C
Credit of returns on this invoice							D
Business related costs							
Number of miles driven in car							
Miles x 0.45							E
Other Travel costs							E
Purchase of other sales materials							E
Telephone costs							E
Internet/broadband costs							E
Printer costs							E
Clothing							E
Marketing/Advertising							E
Postage							E
Accountancy and professional costs							E
Bank costs/processing fees							F
Avon direct delivery fees							F

Campaign Summary

	Order 1 £	Order 2 £	Order 3 £	Order 4 £	Order 5 £	**This Camp £**	
Turnover/Sales							F
Cost of Sales							G
Gross Profit/(Loss)							H
Administrative Expenses							I
Financial Expenses							J
Net Profit							K

Self Assessment Workings - MILEAGE LOG

Date	Destination/Route	Reason	Total Miles	Cum. Total
Mileage Log				

Self Assessment Workings - MILEAGE LOG

Date	Destination/Route	Reason	Total Miles	Cum. Total

Self Assessment Workings - MILEAGE LOG

Date	Destination/Route	Reason	Total Miles	Cum. Total

Self Assessment Workings - MILEAGE LOG

Date	Destination/Route	Reason	Total Miles	Cum. Total

Self Assessment Workings - TIMESHEET **Month:**__________

Date	Description	Total Minutes	Cum. Total
	To calculate hours & minutes divide by 60		

Self Assessment Workings - TIMESHEET **Month:** __________

Date	Description	Total Minutes	Cum. Total
	To calculate hours & minutes divide by 60		

Self Assessment Workings - TIMESHEET

Month: __________

Date	Description	Total Minutes	Cum. Total
	To calculate hours & minutes divide by 60		

Self Assessment Workings - TIMESHEET **Month:** ___________

Date	Description	Total Minutes	Cum. Total
	To calculate hours & minutes divide by 60		

Printed in Poland
by Amazon Fulfillment
Poland Sp. z o.o., Wrocław

60693266R00043